WEBLEY, Ann

The Victorians

D1146136

INTO DRAMA

THE VICTORIANS
ANN WEBLEY

Chrysalis Children's Books

First published in the UK in 2005 by
Chrysalis Children's Books,
An imprint of Chrysalis Books Group,
The Chrysalis Building, Bramley Road, London W10 6SP

Associate Publisher: Joyce Bentley
Editor: Debbie Foy
Art director: Sarah Goodwin
Designer: Angie Allison
Illustrator: Peter Bailey

ISBN 1 84458 327 9

British Library Cataloguing in Publication Data for
this book is available from the British Library.

Printed in Great Britain by
Clays Ltd, St Ives plc

10 9 8 7 6 5 4 3 2 1

CONTENTS

THE VICTORIANS

The Victorian age was a time of invention and change; the fastest change in the history of Britain up to that point.

During the 18th century, most people lived in the countryside and worked on the land. People travelled by horse and cart or by carriage if they were rich. Roads were being improved which made travelling easier, but many people still did not travel far from the place they were born. Most people were unable to read and write and very few had the right to vote.

Queen Victoria's reign brought changes to all of this.
✦ More people worked in factories and mines;
✦ Lots of people moved from the countryside to live in the towns;
✦ The railway meant faster travel in all parts of the country.

These changes were part of what was called the 'Industrial Revolution' and people's lives changed dramatically.

Other important changes happened during this time, too:
✦ By the end of Victoria's reign, more children went to school;
✦ More and more people got the right to vote;
✦ Scientists found out how to treat more diseases;
✦ Inventions changed life inside the home.

SOME IMPORTANT DATES

1837: Queen Victoria came to the throne.

1840: Queen Victoria married Prince Albert.

1848: Public Health Act. (Two more followed in 1872 and 1875.) Towns slowly became cleaner. Sewers were built.

1851: The Great Exhibition was held in London's 'Crystal Palace', so-called because the building was made almost entirely of glass.

1861: Prince Albert died of typhoid.

1867: Men who lived in towns got the right to vote. (Women could not vote until 1918.)

1870: Board schools were set up for all children. There was a fee to pay, so not all children went to school.

1871: The Royal Albert Hall was opened in London in memory of Prince Albert.

1891: Primary education became free.

1897: Queen Victoria's Diamond Jubilee celebrated the fact that she had been Queen for 60 years.

1902: Queen Victoria died.

BOOKS YOU MAY HAVE HEARD OF

You may know of these famous stories. They were written during Queen Victoria's reign.

***Oliver Twist* by Charles Dickens (1838)** An orphan called Oliver runs away, falls in with a gang of thieves in London but finds a proper home in the end.

***The Water Babies* by Charles Kingsley (1863)** Tom, a young chimney sweep, falls into some water and meets some very unusual people.

***Alice's Adventures in Wonderland* by Lewis Carroll (1865)** Alice falls down a rabbit hole and meets a host of amazing characters including a White Rabbit, a Mad Hatter, a Cheshire Cat and a rather scary Queen of Hearts.

***Black Beauty* by Anna Sewell (1877)** This is the story of a horse. Anna Sewell did not like the way horses were treated so she wrote this book to let people know about it.

***Treasure Island* by Robert Louis Stephenson (1883)** A cabin boy called Jim Hawkins meets pirates, including Long John Silver, and has many exciting adventures.

***The Jungle Book* by Rudyard Kipling (1894)** The story of Mowgli the man-cub, and all his animal friends.

FAMOUS VICTORIANS

You might like to find out some more about these people.

Queen Victoria:
+ Started a diary when she was 13 and continued it until her death;
+ Became Queen when she was 18;
+ Married her German cousin, Albert;
+ Had nine children – four sons and five daughters – and 37 grandchildren!

Florence Nightingale:
+ Led a team of nurses to help the injured soldiers in the Crimean War (1854–56);
+ Brought proper medical supplies and made sure everything was clean;
+ Was named 'the Lady of the Lamp';
+ Changed nursing and made it an acceptable job for women.

Isambard Kingdom Brunel:

✦ Was a great engineer
during the Industrial
Revolution;

✦ Designed many bridges,
such as the Clifton
Suspension Bridge
in Bristol;

✦ Designed ships, such as
the *Great Western* and
the *Great Britain*.

Elizabeth Fry:

✦ Visited prisons and was shocked by the dreadful conditions;

✦ Formed a group to help women prisoners and educate
their children.

Charles Darwin:

✦ Wrote a famous book called *The Origin of Species* in 1859;

✦ Claimed that humans may have descended from apes –
this shocked many Victorians.

Lord Shaftesbury:

✦ Worked hard to get laws passed to stop children working in
factories, mines and up chimneys.

TOM'S WORLD

*My name is Tom and I am a climbing boy.
I work for Alf Squabbers who is a master sweep.
There are lots of boys like me cleaning chimneys in
London and most of us are between five and ten years
old. Some come from the workhouses. I didn't. I lived
with my family until I was six, then I was sold to Alf for
20 shillings [£1]. There were too many
of us children and my parents didn't
have enough money to feed us all.*

*Once a year, on 1 May, all the climbing
boys have a wonderful time. We paint
ourselves with a white powder –
it's called being in our
'lilly-whites' – and we
all parade through the
streets, shouting 'weep weep'
and banging our brushes and
climbing tools together!*

William Blake wrote a poem called *The Chimney Sweep*:

When my mother died I was very young,
And my father sold me while yet my tongue
Could scarcely cry 'weep!' 'weep!', 'weep!' 'weep!'
So your chimneys I sweep, and in soot I sleep.

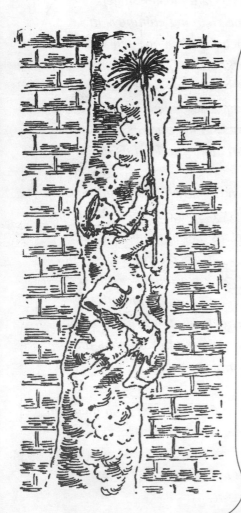

Sweeping chimneys is a dangerous job. The flues are narrow and twisted so you have to be small. That's why the master sweeps want young boys. Before we climb, we rub our skin with brine [salt water] to harden our elbows and knees. It really stings!

This is what can happen to us climbing boys:

✦ *We are pushed up the flue and fires are lit underneath us to make us keep going;*
✦ *Pins are stuck in our feet when we stop for a rest;*
✦ *Soot falls down, making us choke – some boys die of suffocation.*

Once I swept 78 chimneys in three days!

This is how a climbing boy was described at the time: 'He is now 12 years of age, a cripple on crutches, hardly three feet, seven inches [107cm] in stature ... His feet felt like a hog's bristle and his head like a warm cinder ...'

In 1832, a law said that there could be no climbing boys younger than ten years of age, but it was ignored. Lord Shaftesbury worked hard to do something about it and, finally, in 1875, boys were no longer sent up chimneys.

I live with Alf, the master sweep and his family now. Our street has two rows of tenements with cellars. Some of Alf's neighbours have got ten children, and they are all crammed into one or two rooms. The children share beds and sleep at both ends.

We collect our water from a tap in the street and from the river. We share an outside toilet – this is a seat built over a deep pit. Boy, does it smell! The waste in our pit is collected after dark. Apparently, the waste gets sold to farmers who put it on their fields to help their crops grow!

The houses were often dark, damp and stale smelling. People thought that fresh air was unhealthy. One of the most unpleasant jobs must have been that of the 'night soil man'. He came around with his horse and cart at the dead of night, shovelled up all the waste from the pits below the shared toilets and took it away.

TYPICAL DIET FOR A POOR FAMILY

In Victorian times, poor people ate a very unhealthy diet. The food that the poor ate did not contain the vitamins and minerals needed to help fight disease.

This grub doesn't look too bad, does it? But most of the time I just get the bread and cheese. Fat climbing boys are no good to anyone!

Bread and dripping

Potatoes

Cheese

Bacon

Tea with no milk

The poet Edward Lear wrote this limerick about food:

There was an old person of Ewell,
Who chiefly subsisted on gruel;
But to make it more nice,
He inserted some mice,
Which refreshed that old person of Ewell.

There was a great deal of illness among the poor and the death rate was high. It is amazing to think:

✦ Most people died before they were 40;

✦ Between 150 and 160 babies in every thousand died
  before they were a year old.

There were no injections against infectious diseases so these spread very fast, especially among the poor because they all lived so close together. Many people died from measles, smallpox and tuberculosis (a serious disease of the lungs).

However, the biggest problems were caused by the lack of clean water. There were frequent outbreaks of cholera and typhoid which killed many people – even the rich.

Changes began slowly. In 1848, the first Public Health Act set up local Boards of Health to try to make changes. In 1855, the Victorians discovered that cholera was caused by drinking dirty water and the first sewer was built in London in 1865. Gradually, sewers were built all over London and in other towns and cities. At last, clean water could be piped into people's homes. Town councils also had to start collecting rubbish and re-build slum areas to help stop disease spreading.

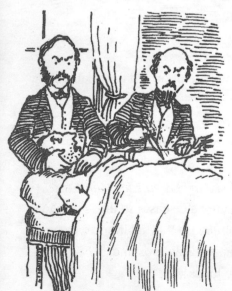

The early Victorians knew very little about treating illness. Doctors used methods such as:

✦ Leeches to suck blood;
✦ Red-hot irons on raw wounds;
  They also wore ordinary clothes to perform operations. They did not realise that cleanliness stopped germs spreading.

As there were no anaesthetics to send patients to sleep during surgery, they often died of shock.

However, important changes took place in medicine in Victorian times:

✦ In 1847, a Scottish doctor, named James Simpson, used chloroform for the first time to put a patient to sleep.

✦ In 1865, Joseph Lister used antiseptic spray to kill germs during an operation.

Despite all the improvements in clean water and medicine, the average life expectancy was only 46 when Queen Victoria died.

You've got the picture – there is a lot of death and illness about. Though I'm only young, I've seen a few 'paupers' funerals'. Poor people who can't afford a proper funeral are buried in a public graveyard. They share the grave with, maybe, 20 others. At the local graveyard, I've even seen bodies start to poke through the earth! There's a terrible smell, as well. There is no church service and no headstone on the grave.

I may not live at home but I still see my parents from time-to-time. My mother works in a laundry. She has a hard life. Washing has to be collected from the posh houses on Monday and returned by Thursday. You should see the state of her hands. They are red raw from scrubbing!

These well-off folks have very fancy clothes and the first thing my mother has to do is take off the ribbons, buttons and lace so they don't get spoiled when she scrubs them hard. Of course, this means it all has to be sewn on again afterwards!

The washerwoman – that's my mother – has to:
◆ Soak the clothes in hot soapy water to loosen the dirt;
◆ Use a 'dolly' or washboard to remove the stains;
◆ Soap the clothes with soda crystals and yellow soap.

After that, she has to starch and dry the clothes and then iron them. Mother uses a flat iron that is heated up on a fire. Flat irons cool down quickly so she has to keep re-heating it. As I said, it's a hard life and it's really tough on her back to keep stooping over that washboard. And there's hardly a day when she's not working.

I don't go to school but there are schools for poor boys run by the church, with a hundred pupils to a class. There are also 'Ragged schools' run by charities – you can imagine why people give them that name! But there are thousands of children on the streets of London who work every day. That is because the children have to work to help the family. Learning to read isn't going to be much good if you haven't got enough to eat!

When I get a chance, I play marbles in the street with my friends. We use the glass stoppers from bottles. One of the girls I know plays with a doll made out of the sole of a shoe. It's got clothes on and a face fixed onto the leather!

Church schools taught the '3Rs' (reading, writing and arithmetic), drill (or PE) and religion for a small fee, but many working people could not afford these basic fees and had to send their children out to work. If there were no church schools, children could go to a 'Dame school'. Old ladies used their parlour as a small schoolroom. Teachers had little or no training in those days and older pupils were used to teach younger ones.

> *I've got lots of friends on the streets of London.*
> *Many of them work as errand boys at the great London*
> *markets: Covent Garden, Smithfield and Billingsgate.*
> *At dawn every morning, crowds of children make their way*
> *to the markets and try to get jobs from the costermongers*.*
> *Can you imagine the noise and bustle?*
>
>
>
> *I've got other friends who clean up horse manure on the streets.*
> *Some hold horses' heads while posh folk go about their*
> *business. Others carry trunks and parcels. There's a lot of*
> *work to do if you go and look for it.*

Unlike Tom, some of these children actually lived on the streets. The Victorians called them 'little arabs' and thought of them as savages. The new Poor Law rules in 1834 meant that if you were fit you could only get food and help inside a workhouse – like the one Oliver Twist lived in. The conditions inside the workhouses were so awful that people wanted to avoid them at all costs.

> *The 'Peelers' are always on the lookout for poor people like us. They expect us to be up to no good. No-one likes them much. This is what we shout:*
>
> *'I spy blue, I spy black! I spy a Peeler in a shiny hat!'.*

Sir Robert Peel started the police force in 1829. The men were named 'Peelers' or 'Bobbies' after him.

The law was harsh on both adults and children in Victorian times:

- ✦ People were flogged for fairly minor crimes;
- ✦ Children were locked up in adult prisons;
- ✦ Thieves were sent to Australia. This was called being deported;
- ✦ Hangings were held in public and these attracted huge crowds of people all trying to get a good view. If someone had a window which overlooked the scaffold, they would charge spectators to stand by it;
- ✦ If people owed money they went to debtor's prison until the debt was paid.

EDMUND AND ALICE'S WORLD

My name is Edmund ...

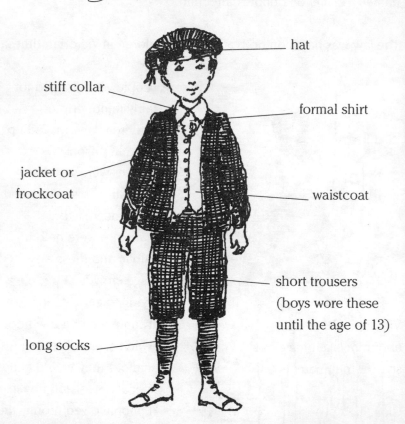

hat

stiff collar

formal shirt

jacket or frockcoat

waistcoat

short trousers
(boys wore these
until the age of 13)

long socks

Boys like Edmund also wore fashionable sailor suits and silk pantaloons for special occasions.

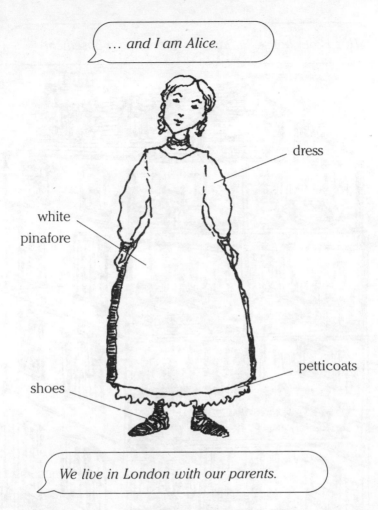

... and I am Alice.

dress

white
pinafore

petticoats

shoes

We live in London with our parents.

Victorian children (boys as well as girls) wore simple dresses until
about the age of five or six. After that, they were dressed in a similar
style to their parents.

Girls like Alice would start to wear a corset from about the age of
13. This was a stiff bodice made from strips of whalebone and was
worn to help keep the waist slim.

This is our house. It has four floors and a basement.

ATTIC
Bedroom – for the parlour maid

TOP FLOOR
Day nursery – where children play and young girls take their lessons
Night nursery – where children sleep
Bedrooms – for the servants

SECOND FLOOR
Master bedrooms – where the gentleman and lady of the house sleep

FIRST FLOOR
Drawing room – where the gentleman and lady of the house entertain their friends

GROUND FLOOR
Entrance hall
Dining room – where the family take their meals
Parlour – where the lady of the house may sit in the mornings

BASEMENT
Kitchen
Stairs for tradesmen

top hat

cravat

great
coat

boots

walking cane

This is our papa,
William Hutchinson.
He is the head of our family and
everyone does what he says. He
can be quite strict. He goes to
work every day in an office in the
City of London. When I grow up
I'm going to work in an office –
or I might become an officer in
the army. I haven't decided yet.

When Papa comes home he likes
Alice and me to tell him what we
have learned during the day.

Papa has a nice singing voice.
In the evenings we sometimes
gather round the piano. Mama
plays and papa sings. Alice and I
join in as well. She is learning
the piano at the moment.

Victorian ladies like Mrs. Hutchinson wore many layers of clothes.
First they put on a chemise, a shapeless undergarment which came
to below the knees. Next, they were laced into a corset. An under-
petticoat, a hooped petticoat and an over-petticoat, with an
embroidered hem, came next. The floor-length dress and other
clothing went on over the top of all this!

This is our mama, Mrs Hutchinson.
Mama does not go out to work. She spends her time doing needlework and embroidery, playing instruments and entertaining. She is the mistress of the house and gives orders to the servants.

bonnet

gloves

long-fitting sleeves

floor-length dress with fancy bodice

three-flounced skirt

button-up boots

Until 1882, a married woman's property belonged to her husband. She could not own anything herself. She was not expected, or even allowed, to work. This is why Florence Nightingale's parents were so upset when she went off to the Crimea with her nurses.

Edmund and I have lots of toys
and games in our nursery.

We have musical boxes
and toy soldiers.

This is my doll.
Her head, arms and legs are made out
of china and her body is made of cloth
and stuffed with sawdust. She has lots
of beautiful clothes to wear. I also have
tiny dolls that live in the dolls' house.

We make up
plays sometimes
and perform them
in our cardboard theatre.

This is a phenaskistoscope.
The figures whirl around
and seem to be moving.

This rocking horse has been in the nursery for years. It is dapple-grey, made of wood and has a mane and tail made from real horse's hair.

When we go outside, we play with hoops, spinning tops, balls and marbles.

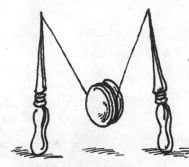

Edmund has a new toy – a leather bell called a diabolo. Some people call it 'a devil on two sticks'.

Alice and I have a favourite game. It is called 'spillikins'. We have a set made of ivory and the spills are all in the shape of weapons. This is how to play:

1. Each player takes one spillikin.
2. The rest are scattered. Do this by holding them all upright in one hand and then letting go of them.
3. Player 1 tries to pull a spill out of the group using his own spill or his fingers. If he moves another one by mistake, his turn is over. If he can remove one without moving any others, he has another go – and keeps going until he makes a mistake.
4. Now it's the turn of player 2, and so on.
5. The winner is the player with the most spillikins at the end. It is quite hard but a lot of fun.

I go to school. There is a public school quite near our house so I can go each day. Some boys board at school and do not see their families so often.

I learn reading, writing and arithmetic. I also learn history and geography. We have to learn lots of facts and chant them out loud when the master tells us. I have also started to learn Latin and Greek and I can read these quite well, now. We write with chalk on slates.

In Victorian schools, learning facts was seen to be more important than imagination and creativity.

Schools were very strict. Lateness might be punished by caning the fingers in front of the whole school. Names were put into a 'disgrace book'. The Victorians did not believe in talking problems through. A well-known Victorian saying went: 'For bad boys, a yard of strap is worth a mile of talk.'

Teachers at the public schools were poorly paid with little formal training. Bullying was common in Victorian times and nobody did anything about it. Younger boys acted as 'fags' for older ones in boarding schools: cleaning shoes, making tea and generally acting as servants.

Edmund goes out to school but Miss Clatworthy, my governess, teaches me in the nursery at home. She has taught me to read and write but I don't have to learn Latin or Greek because girls don't need to know such things. Sometimes she tells me stories about people in the past and I enjoy listening to them.

I also learn to play the piano, to paint and to press flowers and make them into home-made cards to send to our friends. I am also learning cross-stitch so I can embroider samplers like Mama. Miss Clatworthy does not teach me to cook or look after the house. She says this is because I will marry, like my Mama, and have servants to do those things for me.

There were very few schools for rich girls and most were taught at home, like Alice. However, from the 1840s, women like Emily Davies, Dorothea Beale and Frances Buss worked hard to get equal rights for girls and set up schools that they could go to. Miss Beale became headmistress of Cheltenham Ladies' College and Miss Buss ran The North London Collegiate School.

A rather unkind rhyme tried to say that Miss Buss and Miss Beale were not behaving normally by putting all their efforts into educating girls.

> *Miss Buss and Miss Beale*
> *Cupid's darts do not feel.*
> *How different from us,*
> *Miss Beale and Miss Buss.*

Religion is very important in our family life. We say prayers every day at home (usually before meals) and the servants often join in. On Sundays we all go to church at least once. Sometimes we go two or three times during the day. The sermon is always very long but we have to sit still in the pew and we get into trouble if we fidget.

Papa sits and reads aloud to us from the Bible on Sundays. Alice and I have to play very quietly and we are not allowed to play with our usual toys. We have a wooden Noah's ark with lots of painted animals. We are allowed to play with this on Sundays because it is about a Bible story. We can also read other stories from the Bible.

This way of spending Sunday would not have seemed at all strange to the Hutchinson family. Sunday was a day of rest and prayer. Shops and places of entertainment were closed. Families might go for a walk together but the children would not play outdoor games as they might on other days of the week.

Papa says we might be able to go on an outing to the seaside soon. You can get there easily now by train.

Families, like the Hutchinsons, wore their 'Sunday best' to go to the seaside. They stayed covered up even on the hottest days. They enjoyed walking along the promenade. These were built in seaside towns so that visitors could breathe in the sea air without having to walk on the sand.

Another popular activity was a walk along the pier. Many piers had bandstands at the end and chairs so that people could sit and listen to the music.

'Punch and Judy' shows began to appear to entertain children. There were even donkey rides, though children rode the animals in all their heavy clothes!

Some people started to swim in the sea. Men and women always swam separately and they were pushed towards the water in special bathing huts so they did not have to walk across the sand in their bathing costumes. It was very different to a day at the seaside today!

MARY'S WORLD

*I am Mary, Mrs. Hutchinson's parlour maid.
I come from a poor family but I am very lucky because
now I work as a live-in servant. Lots of my friends and
family have much worse jobs than me.*

I've made myself a simple, cotton dress to wear in the mornings when I do most of my cleaning work and I wear the uniform you can see here in the afternoons. I also wear this if I help out and wait at the table when Mr and Mrs Hutchinson have guests to dinner.

Mr Benton, the butler, wears a dark suit all the time, though he takes off the jacket when he is 'below stairs'. He's got a big apron that he puts on when he cleans the family's silver.

I'm always very busy and get rather tired because I work between 15 and 18 hours a day. I get half a day off a week.

I have to behave myself and I'm not allowed any boyfriends. Mrs. Hutchinson is also very strict about servants being honest. Once she put a coin under the carpet to test out a new maid. The silly girl pocketed the money and got dismissed!

Conditions of work would vary. Some people, like the Hutchinsons, treated their servants well. But others were not so thoughtful. Junior maids earned between £9 and £14 a year. Upper servants, such as a cook, earned between £15 and £25 a year. Board and lodging came with the job.

In 1871, over a third of British women between the ages of 12 and 20 were 'in service'. Most servants were women, though many houses employed men as butlers, footmen or gardeners.

I get up at 6am and my first job is to clean the fireplaces. I take my 'maid's box' around from room to room as I do this. In the box, I keep all the things I need to clean and polish the grates: brushes, cloths, emery papers and black lead. The black lead is used to make the grates shiny in the winter when the fires are lit. In the summer, I paint the grate with a home-made varnish made with linseed and turpentine.

Doing the fireplaces is a difficult job. There are always layers of soot each day because of the coal fires, the candles and the oil lamps. It all has to be cleaned – only to get dirty again at once!

Half a million people worked in coalmines to get the coal needed to heat homes, fuel factories and run trains. Smoke pollution in Victorian times was very bad. Towns and cities were often covered in 'smogs', known as 'pea-soupers' because people couldn't see more than a few metres in front of them. The smogs were yellow in colour because of the sulphur given off when the coal burned and a bad one could last for days. They filled the house with a smoky haze and a terrible smell and made it all the more difficult to clean.

Apart from the fires and grates, I have a lot of other jobs to do. Here are just some of them:

✦ *There are ornaments everywhere, so there is a lot of dusting to do. I use a duster made from real feathers;*

✦ I polish all the furniture and the wooden floors. I spend a lot of time on my knees. Now I know why they call hard and painful knees 'housemaid's knee'!;

✦ Most of the washing goes to the washerwoman in the laundry once a week, but that means there is still a lot to do myself each day;

✦ I empty the chamber pots and make the beds;

✦ Some days I scrub the front steps;

✦ I have to clean the windows quite often because of the dirt from the smog;

✦ I carry water round the house to wherever it is needed;

✦ When it gets dark, I light the lamps in the drawing room and the candles in the bedrooms.

So you can see – I have a lot to do and I am worn out when I get to bed!

The kitchen is a very important place for all the servants. We call it 'below stairs'. It's a bit dark because we are in the basement. We use the door down the steps. Only the family and visitors use the front door. Mrs Daye, the cook, is in charge here and she usually has girls to help her prepare the food and wash the dishes.

This is the kitchen. It has a flagstone floor. You can see the coal-fire range on the far wall. All the cooking is done on that. It has an oven built into the side and a hot surface on top for kettles of water and pans of vegetables. If I have to iron one of Madam's dresses, I put the iron on the range to heat it up.

Cook works at that large wooden table in the middle of the room. You can see some of the things she uses on that table, like mixing bowls and pastry-cutters. To the right, you can see a shallow stone sink and a cold water tap – the only tap in the house. This is a real luxury – not every house has a tap yet.

Mrs Daye and her girls are busy all day long preparing meals and then clearing up all the pots and pans.

They also have to preserve food to make it last and stop it going bad. For example:

✦ They boil strawberries and other soft fruits with sugar to make jam;

✦ They pickle vegetables such as cauliflowers and onions in vinegar. The lids of the jars are sealed with wax to stop the air getting to the food;

✦ They pot meat, cover it with melted butter and put it in clay containers. They also preserve joints of meat by rubbing salt all over them.

All this preserved food is stored in one of Mrs Daye's larders.

Mrs Daye has a mincing machine. This is quite a new invention. Now there is no waste. Everything – leftover meat or vegetables – gets put through the machine to be turned into another meal. She also makes pastry for pies. She uses moulds to make jellies. All in all, you would be amazed to see what goes on in our kitchen!

Cook buys the food daily from tradesmen who call at the house. The butcher, baker and greengrocer all ride along our street with their horses and carts and call at each kitchen door. The milkman comes along, as well, with two large churns on his cart. He measures out milk into a jug.

The coalman delivers sacks of coal for the kitchen range and the other fires in the house, and Alf and Tom, the sweeps, come to clean the chimneys.

There are even some tradesmen who call to buy things we don't want, such as bones and dripping. They get taken away to be reused. Believe it or not, old tea leaves are sold and apparently used again by poor folks! I know that I am lucky living in this house. I eat a lot better than many poor people. We don't have quite the same food as the family but we never go hungry. The Hutchinsons usually eat four meals a day – breakfast, luncheon (in the middle of the day), afternoon tea and dinner in the evening.

Sometimes Mrs. Hutchinson has a small luncheon if she is by herself and the family have their main meal in the evening. We servants have our large meal at midday. We have things like boiled beef and mutton, rabbit stew, boiled vegetables and lots of bread.

Here are some of the dishes cook has prepared for the family's dinner this week:

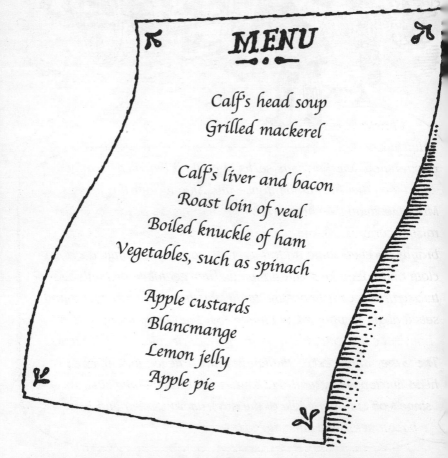

MENU

Calf's head soup
Grilled mackerel

Calf's liver and bacon
Roast loin of veal
Boiled knuckle of ham
Vegetables, such as spinach

Apple custards
Blancmange
Lemon jelly
Apple pie

Christmas is a very busy time of the year in the Hutchinson household – but we all enjoy it because there's always more to eat than usual!

Mrs Daye makes the Christmas pudding well in advance. It has raisins, currants, almonds, lemon peel, eggs, suet, sugar, spices, brandy and beer in it. All this gets mixed together, wrapped in a cloth and boiled for six hours on the range. It is boiled again for two hours on Christmas day. Mr Benton pours brandy over it and sets it alight just before he takes it into the dining room.

The turkey hangs in the larder until it is time to pluck. Then the head is chopped off and any bristles left from the plucking are singed off with twisted paper. The turkey is stuffed with ham, bacon, suet, herbs and breadcrumbs.

Many of our popular Christmas traditions date back to Victorian times:

◆ People decorated their houses with holly and ivy;

◆ They visited each other and enjoyed celebrating Christmas;

◆ They left hand-made 'calling cards', decorated for Christmas;

◆ Many families copied the German tradition and had a Christmas tree. This was often decorated with gingerbread men, marzipan candles and dried fruit as well as wind-up toys and home-made ornaments. A Christmas angel sat at the top.

Like I said before, I'm very lucky compared to some people. Take my cousin Elsie, for example. She lived in the country and she and her husband, Bill, couldn't find work. They decided to move up north to one of the new towns and started work in one of the new cotton mills.

Elsie and Bill set out early to walk to the mill. They take their lunch in a tin with them – usually bread and dripping.

They work long hours and don't earn much, but the worst thing is the danger. Elsie knows people who've had to stop work because they got an arm or leg trapped in the machinery. The dust from the cotton fibres gets in your lungs, too, and makes you cough all the time. Even little children work in the factories and often have to crawl underneath the machines while they are working.

Many people worked hard to improve conditions in factories during the Industrial Revolution:

✦ In 1847 the 'Ten Hours Act' said that women and young people could work no more than ten hours a day.

✦ In 1864, children under eight could no longer work in factories.

✦ Machinery had to be guarded and conditions slowly improved.

INTO THE DRAMA

GETTING READY

You know a lot about the Victorians now, so you are almost ready to perform the play. You could work as a group and act it out as it is written. However, you could also become playwrights yourselves by adding new characters or scenes to the drama to show what you know about Victorian times.

Whichever you choose, there are a lot of jobs for people in your group and you will probably have more than one thing to do!

You need people in charge of:
+ Costumes;
+ Sets;
+ Props;
+ Designing a programme;
+ Music.

You will also need:
+ Actors;
+ A producer (someone who is in charge of putting the whole play together);
+ Writers (if you intend to add to the play).

HOW TO WRITE A PLAY

Read on to get lots of ideas!

✦ Start each scene by describing where the characters are, with details of the time of day and the weather, if those are important. Write this in the present tense, eg **Alice is sitting in the parlour. It is lunchtime**.

✦ Write the names of the characters on the left-hand side of the page (or draw a margin) and use a colon to introduce what they are going to say, eg **Alf: Clean them brushes, lad!**

✦ Never use speech marks or speech verbs, like 'said' or 'replied' in a play.

✦ Use character direction only when necessary. Put this in brackets before the speech. This shows how the words are to be said and helps to bring the character to life, eg **Mary: (in a shocked voice) But what happened to the little boy?**

◆ Think hard about the characters and make their personalities come through in what they say. Make sure they 'stay in character'. In addition, Alf and Tom do not speak in standard English. This helps to show that they are very different from the people who live in the house.

◆ Use stage directions to move the plot along and show what the characters do during the scene, eg **She picks up her maid's box containing cleaning materials and yawns.**

◆ If you are writing on a computer, different colours or fonts can be used to separate the different parts of the writing.

◆ Only use a narrator if it is really necessary.

HOW TO ADD TO THE PLAY

1. Add to a scene

One of the characters could tell the others about:

◆ Somewhere he has been;

◆ A new invention (check the detail first!).

2. Include more characters

✦ In scenes 1 and 3 you could have more servants in the kitchen, such as a scullery maid who washes up and prepares vegetables or an underhouse parlour maid who runs errands;

✦ In scene 4 you could include a younger child or the children's father, Mr Hutchinson.

3. Extend the play

You could do this by:

✦ Starting the play off at Alf's house in the morning before they set out to work;

✦ Adding a scene when the police find Alf and Tom, or when they let them go.

4. Write a new play with the same characters

Here are some ideas:

✦ Write a play with more than one scene about the day the family goes to the seaside;

✦ Write a play set at Christmas time.

5. Change the ending

You could re-write part of the play so there isn't a happy ending for Tom.

MAKING YOUR PLAY REALISTIC

Use detail From Victorian life

If you look carefully at the play in chapter 6, you will get a good idea how this is done.

Notice how details about Victorian life and habits are shown in:

✦ The setting – what is in the room and what the people use;
✦ The jobs people do;
✦ How people speak to each other — look at how people speak to the butler and Mrs. Hutchinson, for example, and try to copy that in your play;
✦ Things that happened in Victorian times. The butler reads from the newspaper about something Lord Shaftesbury is doing. The family are going to the seaside by train.
✦ Mention of real books and poems – the play mentions *Alice in Wonderland*, for example.

If you add to the play, you will be able to use more information from chapters 2, 3 and 4 as well as detail from books in your class or school library.

Use Victorian words and expressions

There are a great number of words and expressions that vary from place-to-place.

Here are some slang expressions
from the London streets:

◆ Crabshells = shoes;
◆ Toff = gentleman;
◆ Bluff = an excuse;
◆ Doxy = wife;
◆ Crib = house;
◆ Back drum = back street;
◆ Armprops = crutches;
◆ Tanner = sixpence (a coin);
◆ Billing and cooing = courting or
    going on a 'date';
◆ Barnacles = spectacles;
◆ Beak = magistrate;
◆ Adam's ale = water;
◆ Belly timber = food.

Villains might use these words:
◆ Dropsy in his pit = money
    in his wallet;
◆ Toby = street robber;
◆ Fagger = small boy who can slip through a window to let
    a burglar in;
But be careful not to use too many or it will sound like a foreign
language to the audience!

Add music

If you want to get more people involved in your play, you could perform some music hall songs at the beginning and end.

In the early part of the 19th century, song and dance acts became popular in many pubs. By the 1880s, the music hall had become as popular as TV is today. There were hundreds in London alone. You would probably have gone every week and enjoyed joining in with all the songs! If you didn't like an act, you booed it off the stage!

Here are the names of some popular Victorian songs. You will be able to find the words and music easily.

- ✦ *Daisy, Daisy;*
- ✦ *Any old iron?;*
- ✦ *Boiled beef and carrots;*
- ✦ *Down at the old Bull and Bush;*
- ✦ *Oh, I do like to be beside the seaside;*
- ✦ *Goodbye-ee.*

Tell jokes

What about trying out some popular Victorian music hall jokes on your audience?

Are your relatives in business?
Yes, they're in the iron and steel business.
Oh, indeed?
Yes – me mother irons and me father steals.

What's the difference between a stoat and a weasel?
I don't know.
A weasel is weasily distinguished.
What about a stoat?
That's stoatally different.

Where were you born?
Liverpool.
What part?
All of me.
Have you lived there all your life?
Not yet.
Any great men born there?
No, only babies.

Do you serve lobsters?
We serve anybody, sir.

PREPARING FOR THE PERFORMANCE

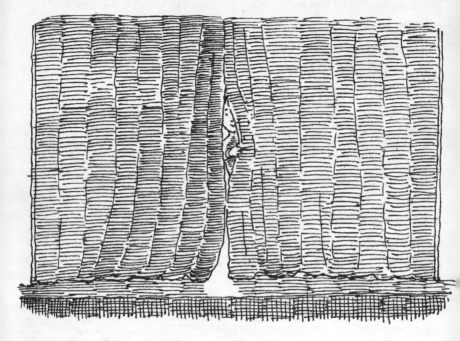

You are nearly ready. You have practised the play and maybe added your own characters or scenes.

You may be performing:
✦ To the class;
✦ To the school;
✦ To your parents.

Depending upon who your audience is and where you are going to perform, you'll need to decide about sets, props and costumes. This can be as simple or as complicated as you like.

Costumes

The simplest way to show a character is to get them to wear a hat or carry a simple prop. For example, the maid could wear a simple white cap or apron. The sweeps could carry brushes. If you want to dress people properly:

✦ Take collars off shirts to make shirts for workers;
✦ Use white sheets to make long aprons;
✦ Use jackets for the butler and Edmund;
✦ Find a way to make a crinoline for Mrs Hutchinson!

You don't have to be good at sewing. Staples and glue can alter clothes quickly, but make sure you get permission and help from an adult before you do anything!

Sets

Again, this can be very simple or much more complicated.

✦ The simplest way is to make a frame and stand different labels against it which tell the audience where the characters are. For

example; **Scene 1: In the kitchen of Mrs Hutchinson's house in London, 1865**. Use classroom tables and chairs for any furniture needed.

✦ If you are using a stage, you could paint a setting onto a white sheet or a roll of corrugated paper. This can be fixed up behind the actors.

You will need people to change the sheet for each new scene. Look at pictures in the books in your classroom and then compare them with the scenes in the play. This will help you decide what to paint.

Props

You need to collect the objects the actors are going to use. It is hard to 'pretend' to clean a grate. It is much easier to have a brush and do it! You won't be able to find real Victorian objects, but it will be easy to find modern equivalents.

For example:
✦ Kitchen objects for scenes 1 and 3;
✦ The necklace that gets lost;
✦ Books for Alice and Edmund;
✦ Sewing for Mrs Hutchinson.

LAST-MINUTE TOUCHES

Your school may be lucky enough to have a stage with lights. If not, you could borrow two portable spot lights from a local secondary school or drama group.

Try to get a microphone on a stand – especially if some of your group have rather soft voices. After all this work, you want the audience to hear you!

Make a programme for the audience. Look at some examples of theatre programmes to find out how to set it out.

If you have included songs, type out the song sheet so the audience can join in.

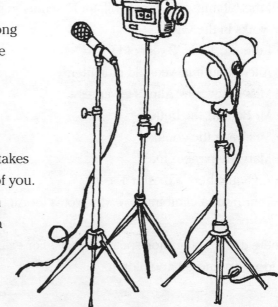

AND FINALLY...

Make sure someone takes lots of photographs of you. Someone might even bring a video camera along.

GOOD LUCK!

THE PLAY

The Missing Necklace

SETTING: Mr and Mrs William Hutchinson's house in a fashionable part of London, 1865.

CHARACTERS:

✦ Mrs Hutchinson, wife of William Hutchinson who
   works in the City;
✦ Edmund, their 12-year-old son;
✦ Alice, their nine-year-old daughter;
✦ Miss Clatworthy, Alice's governess;
✦ Mr Benton, the butler;
✦ Mrs Daye, the cook;
✦ Mary, the parlour maid;
✦ Alf Squabbers, a master sweep;
✦ Tom Trent, a climbing boy who works for Alf.

There can be other non-speaking parts. For example: kitchen maids, a footman and other children.

SCENE 1

In the kitchen, 10am. Mrs Daye is making pastry in a china bowl at a large wooden table in the middle of the room. (Kitchen maids are preparing vegetables and scrubbing the scullery floor.) Mr Benton is reading a newspaper. Mary has just brought in a breakfast tray from Mrs Hutchinson's room.

There is a knock at the kitchen door. Mary opens it.

ALF: Mornin'. Lovely day out there, it is. Come to do the chimneys.

MR BENTON: *(looking up from his paper)* We were expecting
     you tomorrow.

ALF: Ah, yes, well, guv – had to change things, didn't I? My other
     lad got caught in a soot fall. Buried him alive, it did.
     We couldn't do nothing for him. Funeral tomorrow.
     Thought me an' Tom'd better go. Pay our respects, like.

MRS DAYE: That's dreadful, Mr Squabbers! I hope nothing
     like that is going to happen in this establishment.
     (She glances at Tom who is turning his cap around
     in his hands and looking worried.)

ALF: Don't you be fretting, Mary. This lad 'ere will be in and out
     them chimneys before you know it! Can we go through?

MR. BENTON: You need to wait a few minutes, Mr Squabbers.

Mary will go and tell Madam that you are here. You need to cover up the furniture with the sheeting, my girl, before they start. You can clean the rooms as they finish in each one. But don't get behind, now.

MARY: No, Mr Benton. (*She picks up her maid's box containing cleaning materials and yawns.*)

ALF: Tired already, Mary! Out gallivanting last night with a young fella, were you?

MRS DAYE: (*in a shocked voice*) Mr Squabbers, please!
Madam does not like the young girls to go 'gallivanting' as you put it. It's not at all respectable. She's a good worker and she's been working hard since six this morning. She gets the range going for me and is up and about serving the family and cleaning. I dare say she does a lot more than you! Off you go, Mary.

Exit Mary.

MRS DAYE: Do you see much of your mother, Tom?

TOM: Not so much since she sold me to Mr Squabbers two years ago. But she couldn't help it. There was no money, see. All the other little ones. Eight of us there were.
(*Mrs Daye sighs loudly to show disapproval*)

MRS DAYE: Do you ever hear how she is?

TOM: She's fair to middling, thank you kindly, M'am.
Mr Squabbers' neighbour tells me. She's back at the laundry but she finds it so hard. Taking all them frilly bits off the clothes and then doing all that scrubbing on the washboard and pounding with the dolly. Her joints won't stand for it. Me pa's lost his job in the factory.

MR BENTON: What happened?

TOM: Caught his hand in the machine. They fired him.
It's a rum place alright. Fined him for whistling last week they did – though I don't know why anyone'd want to whistle there!

MR BENTON: I've just been reading about Lord Shaftesbury in the morning paper. It seems some more schools for young lads like yourself are going to open in the town. What do you think of that? Would you like to learn to read, Tom?

TOM: Why, Mr Benton, Sir. I don't rightly know. Learning's not for the likes of me. In any case, I got to work for Mr Squabbers.

ALF: Quite right! Don't you be putting ideas in the lad's head.
I never went to school and it never did me no harm.
Lot of do-gooders these toffs!

MR BENTON: I thank you not to talk about your betters in
that way, Mr Squabbers! Mr Shaftesbury is a very kind man.
He tries to make life better for boys like Tom. You should
take a leaf out of his book and treat your boys more kindly.

ALF: (*cheerily*) Right you are, Guv. Can we get on now?

Enter Mary.

MARY: Madam says to start in the drawing room. I've put
the sheets over the chairs.

MR BENTON: Good. You can follow Mary and get on.
Please be very careful. Mrs Hutchinson has some
precious ornaments on the mantelpieces.

MARY: (*Looks back as she goes out of the door*) Oh, Mr Benton,
I nearly forgot. Madam wants me to take one of her
necklaces to the jewellers to have the clasp mended.
Can I go this afternoon?

MR BENTON: That will be quite in order, Mary. Make sure
the cleaning is done first, of course. Madam will want it
mended to wear to the Forsyth's dinner, I'll be bound.

Exit Mary, followed by Alf and Tom.

SCENE 2

The nursery. Alice sits at a desk in the room. Miss Clatworthy is teaching her to embroider.

ALICE: It's no good! I'll never get this right! Ouch! I've pricked
　　　　my finger again. (*She sucks her finger.*)

MISS C: (*soothingly*) Come now, Alice. It isn't like you to give up!
　　　　Learning to embroider is very important for a young lady.
　　　　Your mama will be so pleased with this sampler. You can
　　　　give it to her for her birthday – but not if you get blood on it!

ALICE: I know. And I do so want to please Mama. But it seems
　　　　so difficult. Sometimes I wish I could go to school each
　　　　day like Edmund. I wonder what he's doing now?

MISS C: No doubt he will tell you later, but it wouldn't be at
　　　　all proper for you to go to school. The grammar school is
　　　　for boys. They need to learn Latin and Greek and the like.
　　　　You will get married one day and you will have a fine house
　　　　to run like your dear Mama. (*Alice sighs and continues to
　　　　work on her embroidery.*)

ALICE: What else are we doing today?

MISS C: We must read some more of your book, Alice. You still
　　　　do not read aloud with enough expression.

ALICE: (*whines*) Do we have to? It's sooo boring. I don't
enjoy the story at all!

MISS C: Reading is very important for a young lady, Alice.
However, it so happens that I have found another book you
may enjoy more. (*She takes it off a shelf.*) Look. This was
only published this year. It's by a man called Lewis Carroll.
Apparently he told the story aloud and the little girls enjoyed
it so much that he wrote it down. (*Alice takes the book from
Miss Clatworthy and looks at it.*)

ALICE: (reads) *Alice's Adventures in Wonderland.* Oh!
(*laughs with delight*) She's called Alice, like me. (*opens the
first page and reads*) 'Chapter 1. Down the rabbit-hole. Alice
was beginning to get very tired of sitting by her sister on the
bank, and of having nothing to do; once or twice she had
peeped into the book her sister was reading, but it had no
pictures or conversations in it, "and what is the use of a
book," thought Alice, "without pictures or conversations?"'
(*whining again*) That does not sound very good!

MISS C: Goodness me, Alice! You do give up easily. I have had
a look. There are white rabbits that talk, a mad hatter, a very
odd queen and all manner of interesting characters. I think
it is just the book to practise reading aloud to your Mama!

**There is a knock at the door and Mary enters with Alf
and Tom.**

MARY: Mr Squabbers and Tom are going to do the chimney in here next, Miss Clatworthy. It might be best if you move your lesson to another room. There'll be a lot of soot.

MISS C: Dear, dear! How inconvenient – just when we have all the threads laid out nicely. Still, we don't want to get covered in soot!

ALF: That you don't, Miss. The young lady's fine white pinafore would be right ruined.

Mary puts sheets over the furniture. Miss Clatworthy starts to collect up the embroidery materials. Tom spots something on a shelf.

TOM: (*pointing*) What's that?

ALF: Hold your tongue, you young varmit. It's not your place to talk to the little Miss.

ALICE: (*smiling*) Oh, I don't mind, Mr Squabbers. Don't be cross with him. It's a new toy. Papa says it's called a phen – ak – is – to – scope. (*She talks very slowly to get the name right.*)

TOM: Blimey, Miss! That's a mouthful!

ALICE: Yes – and look. I'll hold it up so you can see. I don't want you to touch it with those filthy hands! (She holds the handle and whirls the disc.) See, those horses look like they are moving!

TOM: That's amazing, Miss. Just like a horse race, it is.

ALF: Come on, boy. Less of the rabbitting. Got to get on.
Two more rooms after this. Are you done, Mary?

MARY: You can go ahead now. I'll get the last two rooms ready.
Be very careful in Madam's bedroom.

**Mary, Alice and Miss Clatworthy exit. Alf and Tom go over
to the fireplace. Alf peers up the chimney.**

ALF: This 'ere'll be a tight 'un. Lucky I don't feed you much!

TOM: That's true. Only bread and dripping this morning. But I
will grow, Mr Squabbers. What'll become of me then?

ALF: Then, my lad, you'll be no use to me. Not my problem. (*His
mood changes and he starts to shout.*) Now get going or
you'll feel this stick on your ungrateful backside!

TOM: My knees hurt!

ALF: Stop yer moaning. Didn't you rub the brine in like I told you?

TOM: 'Course I did. I always do. But it doesn't help.

**Tom moves into the fireplace, holding his brushes, and starts
to climb. No-one talks for a few minutes.**

TOM: (*faintly*) I'm stuck!

ALF: (*angry*) You are causing me a deal of trouble today.
     I'll get you going for sure.

**He lights a taper and sets fire to a few coals that are still
in the hearth. Tom coughs and splutters.**

TOM: Ahh!! Mr Squabbers! Don't! I'm doing my best!

ALF: But it's not good enough, boy!

**Tom wriggles and grunts and pulls himself past the turn
in the chimney.**

TOM: I'm through!

**He works with his brush and a large amount of soot falls
down into the room. Tom and Alf cough. Tom slides back
down, his face covered with soot.**

TOM: There – I did it.

ALF: 'Course you did. Now you get into the Missus' room and
     get on up there while I sweep this lot up.

Exit Tom. Alf carries on sweeping soot up.

SCENE 3

In the kitchen, 12pm. The final preparations for luncheon are being carried out. Mrs Daye checks the pie in the range. She tastes the soup and seasons it.

MRS DAYE: Bless me! It's hot today. I shall be glad when this lot goes upstairs.

MR BENTON: Madam asked for luncheon at one o'clock sharp, Mrs Daye. The table is laid in the dining room.

MRS DAYE: I'll be ready. She wanted chops today. They don't take much cooking. We'll have the cold meat from yesterday, shall we, Mr Benton?

MR BENTON: That would be most acceptable on a hot day. Shall we have some pickles?

MRS DAYE: I'll get a jar out of the larder. I dare say Madam will like cold tomorrow if this heat goes on.

MR BENTON: I think the family are going out on an excursion, Mrs Daye. The Master decided this morning. They are going on the train to Brighton.

MRS DAYE: (*shocked*) Well I never! I'm surprised at Madam – taking the children on those dangerous engines!

MR BENTON: (*laughs*) Come now, Mrs Daye. The railways have
been around for a long time and they are quite safe. The
Master often travels this way, but the children have never
been on a train.

MRS DAYE: (*unconvinced*) That's as maybe but you wouldn't get
me on one. Forty miles an hour! It's a wonder people don't
fall dead on the spot with a heart attack going at that speed!
No, I'll stick to the horse and carriage, thanks all the same.
I don't hold with all this new-fangled nonsense.

Enter Mary looking very upset.

MARY: Oh, Mr Benton, something dreadful has happened!
I think Madam's necklace has been stolen!

MRS DAYE & MR BENTON: STOLEN!!?

Mary starts to cry. Mr Benton hands her a handkerchief.

MR BENTON: Calm yourself, my girl and tell us what has happened.
Is this the necklace you are supposed to be getting mended?

MARY: Yes. I know I picked it up from Madam's dressing table and
I had it in my hand. I think that was just before I took Mr
Squabbers and Tom through to Miss Clatworthy. I'd been in
the rooms on that floor and done all the sheets. I must have
put it down. I'm so stupid! Madam will sack me for sure.

MR BENTON: Very likely. It was a very careless thing to do. But you said it had been stolen. It sounds more like you left it somewhere.

MARY: Yes, I did. I'm sure I did. But you see I have had a look. I can't see it anywhere, but now I remember I saw Tom go along the corridor by himself. Peering at everything, he was.

MRS DAYE: What? Mr Squabbers wasn't with him?

MARY: No. I saw him as I passed the nursery door. They must have brought a load of soot down because he was down on his hands and knees clearing it up. I thought that was nice of him – not leaving it to me, like.

MRS DAYE: So, you think …

MARY: I'm afraid it is Tom. He must have seen it wherever I left it and put it in his pocket.

MR BENTON: I'm afraid you are right, Mary. It doesn't do to let lads like Tom loose in a house such as this. Too much temptation. We know what his life is like. He'll take it to the pawn shop, I'll be bound.

MRS DAYE: But he's such a nice little lad. I can't believe it. He's always ever so polite.

MR BENTON: Well that would be part of the plan, wouldn't it?

Make us all feel sorry for him so we never suspect him.
I wouldn't be surprised if he's not doing it for Squabbers.
They could be a gang. We must call the police.

MRS DAYE: What now? I'm just going to serve the soup!

MR BENTON: No, you're right, Mrs Daye. We don't want to spoil
Madam's luncheon. Mary – you are to go upstairs and look
again in every room. We must make sure the necklace isn't
here. Then if we do not find it, we will tell Madam after she
has eaten.

MARY: Yes, Mr Benton. I will look but I did not see it before.
I'm sure it has been stolen. (*Starts to cry again.*)

MRS DAYE: Be off with you now, girl. You're getting under my feet.

**Mary exits. Mrs Daye spoons the soup into a large china
tureen and puts it on the tray. Mr Benton picks it up and
goes out of the kitchen.**

SCENE 4

**In the drawing room, late afternoon. Mrs Hutchinson is
sewing. The door opens and Edmund and Alice enter.
Edmund carries a pile of books tied together with a leather
strap. Alice has a doll. She sits down on a footstool. Edmund
stands in front of his mother. Mrs Hutchinson looks up from
her sewing.**

MRS H: Ah, children! Just in time for tea! Did you have a good
day at school today, Edmund?

EDMUND: It was alright, Mama. Mr Philips was in a bad mood,
though. Peterson got the cane.

MRS H: Whatever did he do?

EDMUND: He didn't know his Latin verbs. But I knew mine!
(*proudly*) And I got them all right. We are learning the Bible
in Latin, as well.

MRS H: Did you do anything else?

EDMUND: Oh yes. We are learning about the war against Napoleon
and how brave all the soldiers were. We read a poem about
a battle. We started to learn it by heart. I know the first
two verses ...

ALICE: (*interrupting*) I bet it's really boring.

EDMUND: (*Ignores her. He puts his books down and stands to attention ready to recite.*)
Casabianca by Mrs Felicia Dorothea Hemnans, 1829

The boy stood on the burning deck
Whence all but he had fled;
The flame that lit the battle's wreck
Shone round him o'er the dead.

Yet beautiful and bright he stood,
As born to rule the storm;
A creature of heroic blood,
A proud, though childlike form.

(*He bows to show he has finished. Mrs Hutchinson smiles and claps. Alice scowls.*)

ALICE: That doesn't make sense! Why would he stand in the middle of the flames? Didn't he have the sense to run away with everyone else? I've started to read a much better book. Miss Clatworthy found it for me. It's called *Alice's Adventures in Wonderland* so I will imagine that the adventures have happened to me! So far, Alice has fallen down a rabbit hole and followed a white rabbit wearing a waistcoat, who keeps muttering that he is late.

EDMUND: How ridiculous! At least the story in the poem is about a real battle. Rabbits wearing waistcoats are for babies!

MRS H: Stop it at once, Edmund. I expect you to be kind and polite to your sister. Gentlemen do not make fun of other people.

EDMUND: (*glaring at Alice*) Yes, Mama. Sorry, Mama.

ALICE: Mama's necklace was stolen today!

EDMUND: Who by? Was the thief caught?

ALICE: Not yet! It was ever so exciting! Mr Squabbers and Tom came to clean the chimneys. Tom went off on his own and stole the necklace. Mama had to call the police after luncheon and they have gone to find him.

EDMUND: Oh, I wish I had been here. I could have helped in the chase!

MRS H: It was not a chase, Edmund and it was not exciting. It is very upsetting and I just hope the police find the necklace before your Papa gets home because goodness knows what he will say.

EDMUND: (*looking very cheerful*) I expect they will throw Tom in prison or even hang him. I heard Papa say you can't expect the lower classes to know how to behave. They haven't had the education we have.

ALICE: (*looks confused*) I don't think that is a very nice thing to say, Edmund. I think Tom is quite nice.

EDMUND: Yes, well that proves how stupid girls are, doesn't it?

MRS H: Stop arguing, you two. I have one of my heads coming on. I think I will go and lie down. I'm sorry, Alice but you must understand that the boy is a thief and that is the end of it.

There is a knock at the door.

If that is Mary with the tea I think I will have mine in my room. I really don't feel well. (*raises her voice*) Come in.

Enter Mr Benton and Mary who is looking very upset.

MRS H: Yes Mr Benton? Is there any news about my necklace?

MR BENTON: There is, Madam. I have it here.

MRS H: (*cheerily*) Why that is marvellous! The police have done a fine job. Very speedy.

MR BENTON: Well no, Madam. It wasn't the police. I think Mary had better tell you what happened.

MRS H: Well, Mary?

MARY: (*stuttering*) I'm e-e-ever so sorry, M-Madam. I did see Tom Trent go off on his own and when I couldn't find the necklace I just thought it was him. But it wasn't. (*She stops and looks at the floor.*)

MRS H: (*firmly*) Well? Go on, Mary.

MARY: This afternoon I noticed that the drawing room rug still had soot on it. When I lifted it I saw the necklace. It must have been knocked on the floor and pushed underneath. That's why I didn't see it when I searched, Madam.

MRS H: I see. You have been a very foolish girl today, Mary. I trusted you with the necklace. Furthermore, your carelessness has meant that an innocent boy has been accused by the police. I will have to think what to do about you. But there is something more important now. Mr Benton, what can we do about the matter?

MR BENTON: If I may suggest, Madam, you could write a letter explaining that the necklace has been found and I will take it myself to the police station. That should be an end to it.

MRS H: That is a good idea.

She moves to a writing desk by the window, takes some paper and a quill pen and writes the letter. Mr Benton and Mary are silent. Edmund watches; Alice is playing with her doll again. Mrs Hutchinson puts the letter in an envelope and addresses it. She hands it to Mr Benton.

MRS H: Here you are, Mr Benton. Go quickly, now.

Mr Benton exits.

MRS H: Mary, I will want my tea in my room. I have a terrific headache after all the fuss and worry. I will speak to you again, later.

MARY: (*sadly*) Yes, Madam.

She curtsies and goes out.

EDMUND: You should dismiss her, mother!

ALICE: But that's not fair! She found the necklace, didn't she?

EDMUND: But if it wasn't for her, it wouldn't have gone missing in the first place.

MRS H: Children! Please do not argue! I shall recommend to your father that we do not take the excursion tomorrow if you cannot behave better.

EDMUND: Oh, please don't do that, Mama. I am really looking forward to going on the train. Lots of boys at school have been to Brighton and two of them even bathed in the sea!

MRS H: I'm sure we shall all enjoy ourselves. But I have to get rid of this dreadful head first. I am going to have my tea and then lie down. Please go back to the nursery. You can take your tea up there. I will see you before you go to bed.

EDMUND & ALICE: Yes, Mama.

They exit. A moment later Mrs Hutchinson follows.

THE END

GLOSSARY

Board of Health a group of townspeople who tried to improve cleanliness so that people would be healthier.

Butler the main male servant in the house.

Chloroform a substance that used to put people to sleep during an operation.

Cholera an infectious disease that often resulted in death.

Costermonger a person who sells things.

Cotton mill a factory where cotton fibres were woven on machines into cloth.

Dolly used to wash clothes by washerwomen and may have been named because it looked like a simple doll.

Fags younger boys who did jobs for older ones in public schools. They were often bullied.

Governess a lady who taught children at their home.

Industrial revolution a time of great change. More people lived in towns and worked in factories. Railways were built across the country.

Kitchen range cooker and fire.

Leech a worm that sucks blood.

Lilly-whites decoration used by sweeps on first day of May.

Little Arabs a name for the children who lived on the streets.

Night-soil man a man who came at night to collect the waste from the shared pit which was used as the toilet.

Parlour the sitting room or lounge.

Peelers the name for policemen – named after Sir Robert Peel.

Poor Law in 1834 the law was changed to say that no one who was fit and healthy could get help from the Poor Law except in a workhouse.

Ragged school a school for poor children.

Sampler a piece of embroidery, usually in cross-stitch that included a picture and words from the Bible.

Sewer a drain that carries waste and dirty water.

Slums overcrowded buildings for very poor people that were unfit for humans to live in.

Smog a very bad fog caused by pollution from factories and fires.

Tenements rows of terraced buildings divided into separate, very basic homes for the poor.

Typhoid an infectious fever that often resulted in death.

Workhouse a place where poor, able-bodied people worked in return for food and shelter. The conditions were made very bad so that people would not want to live there.

INDEX